20 FUN FACTS ABOUT AMPHIBIAN ADAPTATIONS

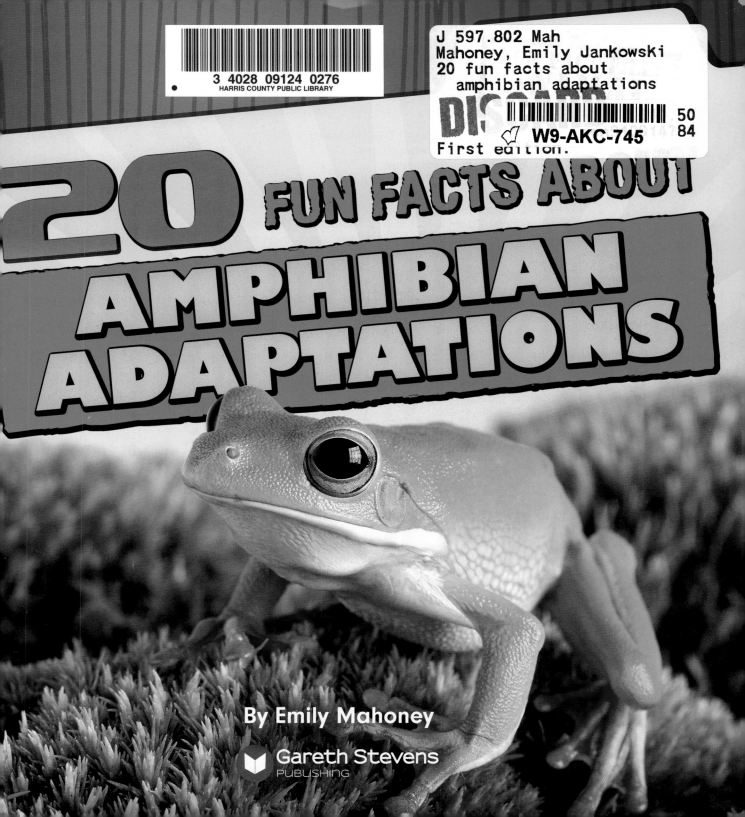

By Emily Mahoney

Gareth Stevens
PUBLISHING

Please visit our website, www.garethstevens.com. For a free color catalog of all our high-quality books, call toll free 1-800-542-2595 or fax 1-877-542-2596.

Library of Congress Cataloging-in-Publication Data

Mahoney, Emily Jankowski, author.
 20 fun facts about amphibian adaptations / Emily Mahoney.
    pages cm. — (Fun fact file. Animal adaptations)
 Includes bibliographical references and index.
 ISBN 978-1-4824-4447-6 (pbk.)
 ISBN 978-1-4824-4391-2 (6 pack)
 ISBN 978-1-4824-4429-2 (library binding)
 1. Amphibians—Miscellanea—Juvenile literature. 2. Adaptation (Biology)—Juvenile literature. 3. Children's questions and answers. I. Title. II. Title: Twenty fun facts about amphibian adaptations. III. Title: Amphibian adaptations.
 QL644.2.M38 2017
 597.802—dc23

                                    2015021550

First Edition

Published in 2016 by
Gareth Stevens Publishing
111 East 14th Street, Suite 349
New York, NY 10003

Designer: Andrea Davison-Bartolotta
Editor: Kristen Nelson

Photo credits: Cover, p. 1 Anneka/Shutterstock.com; p. 4 Christian Vinces/Shutterstock.com; p. 5 (top left) marima/Shutterstock.com; p. 5 (top right) CreativeNature R.Zwerver/Shutterstock.com; p. 5 (middle left) Choke29/Shutterstock.com; p. 5 (middle right, bottom left) Dirk Ercken/Shutterstock.com; p. 5 (bottom right) Tremor Photography/Shutterstock.com; p. 6 Gustav W. Verderber/Getty Images; p. 7 Andrew Sabai/ Shutterstock.com; p. 8 Angel DiBilio/Shutterstock.com; p. 9 Marevision/Getty Images; p. 10 Jason Mintzer/ Shutterstock.com; p. 11 (inset) reptiles4all/Shutterstock.com; p. 11 (main) Cathy Keifer/Shutterstock.com; p. 12 Eric Krouse/Shutterstock.com; p. 13 Gail Shumway/Getty Images; p. 14 Auscape/Getty Images; p. 15 © iStockphoto.com/randimal; p. 16 (bottom) QueSeraSera/Shutterstock.com; p. 16 (top) marcovarro/ Shutterstock.com; p. 18 Joseph T Collins/Getty Images; p. 19 E R Degginger/Getty Images; p. 20 Marek R. Swadzba/Shutterstock.com; pp. 21, 25 Randimal/Shutterstock.com; p. 22 Brandon Alms/Shutterstock.com; p. 23 Damian Money/Shutterstock.com; p. 24 Stacy Gold/Getty Images; p. 26 dabjola/Shutterstock.com; p. 27 paween/Shutterstock.com; p. 28 GlobalP/iStock/Thinkstock; p. 29 John Cancalosi/Getty Images.

Printed in the United States of America

CPSIA compliance information: Batch #CW16GS: For further information contact Gareth Stevens, New York, New York at 1-800-542-2595.

Contents

Awesome Amphibians. .4

Funky Frogs 6

Life in the Trees 10

Toad-ally Cool Survival Skills 14

Salamander Smarts. 18

Nifty Newts 22

A Unique Way of Life. 26

Adaptation Education 28

Glossary. 30

For More Information. 31

Index 32

Words in the glossary appear in **bold** type the first time they are used in the text.

Awesome Amphibians

There are many kinds of amphibians on our planet, including frogs, toads, salamanders, and newts. In fact, there are more than 6,500 species, or types, of amphibians in the world! Some amphibians live in faraway places, while others might live right in your backyard!

Each species has **unique** features called adaptations that help it survive in its **environment**. Without these adaptations, amphibians wouldn't live very long.

The word "amphibian" means "being that leads a double life," which refers to the fact that amphibians spend part of their life in water and part on land.

FACT 1

Wood frogs can freeze and **thaw** as the temperature changes.

Recently, scientists discovered that wood frogs have special **proteins** that cause the water in their blood to freeze before the rest of their body when it's very cold outside. When the air warms up, the ice melts—and they're fine!

Frogs actually "change" their skin once a week to make sure they stay moist, or wet. They do this by pulling the old layer of skin off, like a dirty shirt!

FACT 2

A frog's skin is made to keep it wet.

Have you ever picked up a frog and noticed its slimy skin? There's a thin layer of **mucus** on it. It keeps a frog's skin from drying out, especially if it's in the sun for a long time.

FACT 3

It's hard to sneak up on a frog.

Frogs have large eyes on top of their head that can see in many directions. They have very good eyesight and are able to see things in the darkness other animals might not be able to see.

A frog's eyes help it swallow.

When a frog has caught some prey, it seems to blink while it's eating. Its eyes are actually sinking into its head to push the food down its throat!

Frogs can see in a wide range of colors. Many animals can't see color at all!

FACT 5

The famous frog call "ribbet" is actually the mating call of the Baja California tree frog.

In order to find a mate, male tree frogs make a special sound. Each frog species' mating call is unique. Female frogs know what their species' call sounds like and listen for it!

Some tree frogs use just their tongue to catch prey.

A tree frog's tongue is very long and is sticky on the end. This allows the frog to catch prey that's moving very fast. This can take less than a second!

Some tree frogs are brightly colored to warn predators they're poisonous.

FACT 7

A tree frog's toes are so sticky it can climb on glass.

Tree frog feet need to be supersticky so the frogs don't fall out of trees! Their feet have tiny, hairlike body parts scientists call "nanopillars" that work with mucus on their feet to make their feet stick.

Tree frogs sometimes look like they're flying when they jump through the air!

Tree frogs can jump over 20 times their own length!

A tree frog's legs are very long in order to let it jump from branch to branch in trees. They're also very powerful. In fact, the length of the frog's jump can be compared to you jumping 100 feet (30.5 m)!

Toad-ally Cool Survival Skills

FACT 9

Toads ooze a toxin, or poison, out of their skin to hurt their predators.

In order to keep from getting eaten, toads can let poison out onto their skin. It oozes out when the toad feels like it's in danger. Some kinds of toads' poison can really harm people, too!

You can see the poison oozing from this cane toad's skin!

Some desert toads have extra "toes" to help them dig.

Desert animals have adaptations because their **habitat** is so hot and dry. The Couch's spadefoot toad uses a hard body part called a spade on its back foot to dig in the sand to hide from predators, keep out of the **harsh** sun, and find water underground.

spade

Frogs and toads are similar animals, but toads have some different adaptations that help them survive in dry environments.

Many toads live in North America, so you've probably seen one!

FACT 11

Most toads are colored to blend in with the dirt, mud, or sand that they live on.

In order to blend in with their environment, many toads are different shades of brown. This means that when predators are

looking for them, they're tricky to find. Toads have bumpy skin, too, which also helps them hide in their environment.

Frogs and Toads

frogs

live in wet environments

slimy skin

narrow body

long back legs

both

amphibians

hatch from eggs

may let poison **chemicals** out of their skin

eat insects

toads

live in dry environments

bumpy, rough skin

wide body

short back legs

FACT 12

A salamander can regenerate, or regrow, its tail.

A salamander is an amphibian that looks somewhat like a lizard and commonly lives in wet environments. If a predator catches a salamander by its tail, its tail will **detach** so that the salamander can escape.

This salamander's tail is just starting to regrow after it was lost.

mudpuppy

Mudpuppy salamanders can regrow legs and even parts of their brain!

The mudpuppy salamander is a special kind of salamander because in addition to its tail, it can regenerate its legs. Sometimes, a leg starts to grow as another one is healing, so mudpuppies may have *extra* legs!

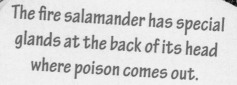

The fire salamander has special glands at the back of its head where poison comes out.

FACT 14

A salamander's colors are an adaptation that warns predators to stay away!

Brightly colored animals are commonly poisonous. The fire salamander has bright yellow markings to warn predators of this fact. Other salamanders are bright orange or red, and the colors mean the same thing: Don't eat me!

Female salamanders can lay up to 200 eggs at one time.

When a female spotted salamander lays her eggs, they have a jellylike layer around them. The jelly keeps the eggs safe from predators and makes them more likely to hatch into baby salamanders.

FACT 16

Newts are dark colors so they can't be seen at night.

Newts are nocturnal, which means they have adapted to sleeping during the day and being most active at night. Pet newts should be kept in low light because of this adaptation, too.

Newts are a kind of salamander that spends some of its time living on land.

FACT 17

Newts breathe through their skin.

Newts **evolved** to use their watery home to hide from predators. Breathing through their skin means that newts don't need to come out of the water. They can stay hidden when a predator is nearby.

Some newts might know how to follow directions.

Scientists have been studying the effect of Earth's **magnetic field** on newts. It seems that newts know where their home is based on differences in the magnetic field! More studies are needed to learn more about this ability.

If a person swallowed the rough-skinned newt, they would be poisoned and die.

Like many other amphibians, newts give off toxins through their skin. The alligator newt pushes its ribs through its skin to stick poison into predators! Newts are poisonous in all stages of their life cycle.

Newts can live 15 years or more!

A Unique Way of Life

tadpoles

FACT 20

Amphibians have a unique life cycle.

Amphibians lay eggs; tadpoles hatch from the eggs. As the tadpoles grow, their body changes, and then the tadpoles grow into full-sized frogs, newts, toads, or salamanders. It can take up to a few years for this life cycle to be complete.

Female amphibian
lays eggs

Adult amphibians grow

Tadpoles hatch
from eggs

Tadpoles grow limbs
and lungs

Adaptation Education

From detachable tails to poisonous skin, amphibians are cool creatures! Since they're found all over the world, they must be able to adapt to a wide variety of environments in order to survive.

Many people keep amphibians as pets because of their beauty. Since they can be kept in tanks or cages, they're commonly easy to care for as well. Knowing about amphibian adaptations will allow you to appreciate just how unique they really are!

Argentine horned frog